I0820614

a Little Golden Book® BIOGRAPHY

DOLLY PARTON

ULTIMATE FAN EDITION

Golden Books
An imprint of Random House Children's Books
A division of Penguin Random House LLC
1745 Broadway, New York, NY 10019
penguinrandomhouse.com
rhcbooks.com

Originally published in a slightly different form as *Dolly Parton: A Little Golden Book Biography* by Golden Books, an imprint of Random House Children's Books, a division of Penguin Random House LLC, New York, in 2021.
Library of Congress Control Number: 2025936224
ISBN 979-8-217-22330-5 (trade)
Manufactured in the United States of America
10 9 8 7 6 5 4 3 2 1
The authorized representative in the EU for product safety and compliance is
Penguin Random House Ireland, Morrison Chambers, 32 Nassau Street, Dublin D02 YH68, Ireland.
https://eu-contact.penguin.ie

a Little Golden Book® BIOGRAPHY

DOLLY PARTON

ULTIMATE FAN EDITION

By Deborah Hopkinson

Illustrated by Monique Dong

A GOLDEN BOOK • NEW YORK

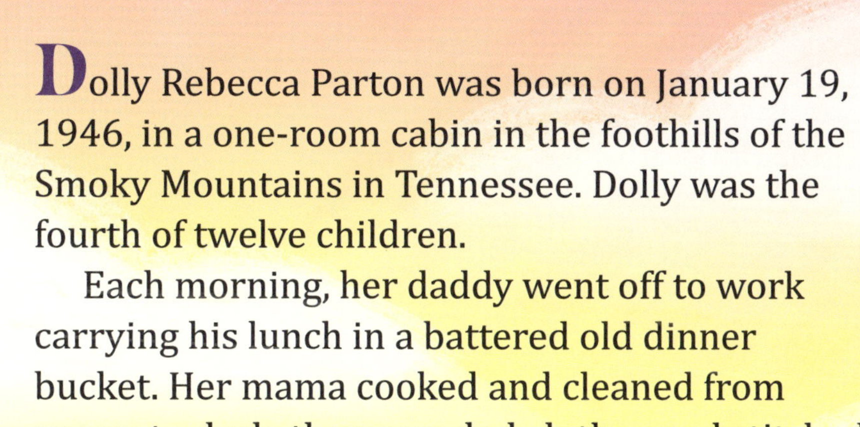

Dolly Rebecca Parton was born on January 19, 1946, in a one-room cabin in the foothills of the Smoky Mountains in Tennessee. Dolly was the fourth of twelve children.

Each morning, her daddy went off to work carrying his lunch in a battered old dinner bucket. Her mama cooked and cleaned from sunup to dark, then mended clothes and stitched quilts by the light of a kerosene lamp. Her family might have been poor, but Dolly's life was rich with music and love.

Dolly and her sisters and brothers made their own fun. From the time she was little, Dolly pretended she was a star. She perched on the woodpile or stood on the cabin porch to perform for the chickens, the ducks, and her little brothers and sisters. Sometimes, though, her audience just crawled off or waddled away.

One chilly fall, Dolly's mama made her a special coat from colorful scraps of cloth. Kids at school called it a bunch of rags. Their teasing made Dolly sad, but she wouldn't take off her coat. She knew her mama had sewn each tiny stitch with love.

When she grew up, Dolly told this story in her famous song "Coat of Many Colors."

Dolly has always loved butterflies, flitting and flying so free. One day when she was a child, she followed a bright-orange monarch and got lost in the woods.

Suddenly, she heard a bell. It was the family cow, Bessie! Dolly ran over and grabbed the leather collar her daddy had made for the animal. Dolly hung on tight, stumbling through briars and bushes as Bessie led her all the way home.

Dolly is a bit like a beautiful butterfly herself—gentle and colorful. She lights up the stage in her fancy outfits. And she enjoys showing off her gorgeous, glamorous wigs.

Even though she's all grown up, Dolly still makes her own fun.

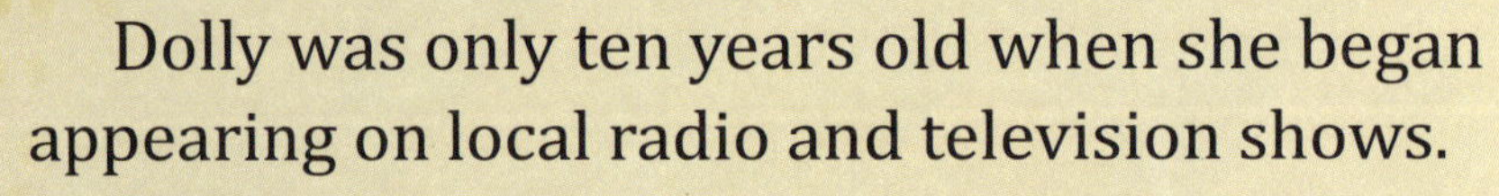

Dolly was only ten years old when she began appearing on local radio and television shows.

At first, she felt nervous. Then she took a big breath and sang from her heart, just like at home on the woodpile. Her dazzling smile and clear, high voice charmed everyone.

Dolly was on TV before her family even owned one!

As a girl, Dolly set her sights high. She dreamed of singing onstage at the famous Grand Ole Opry in Nashville. From there, people all over America would hear her on their radios.

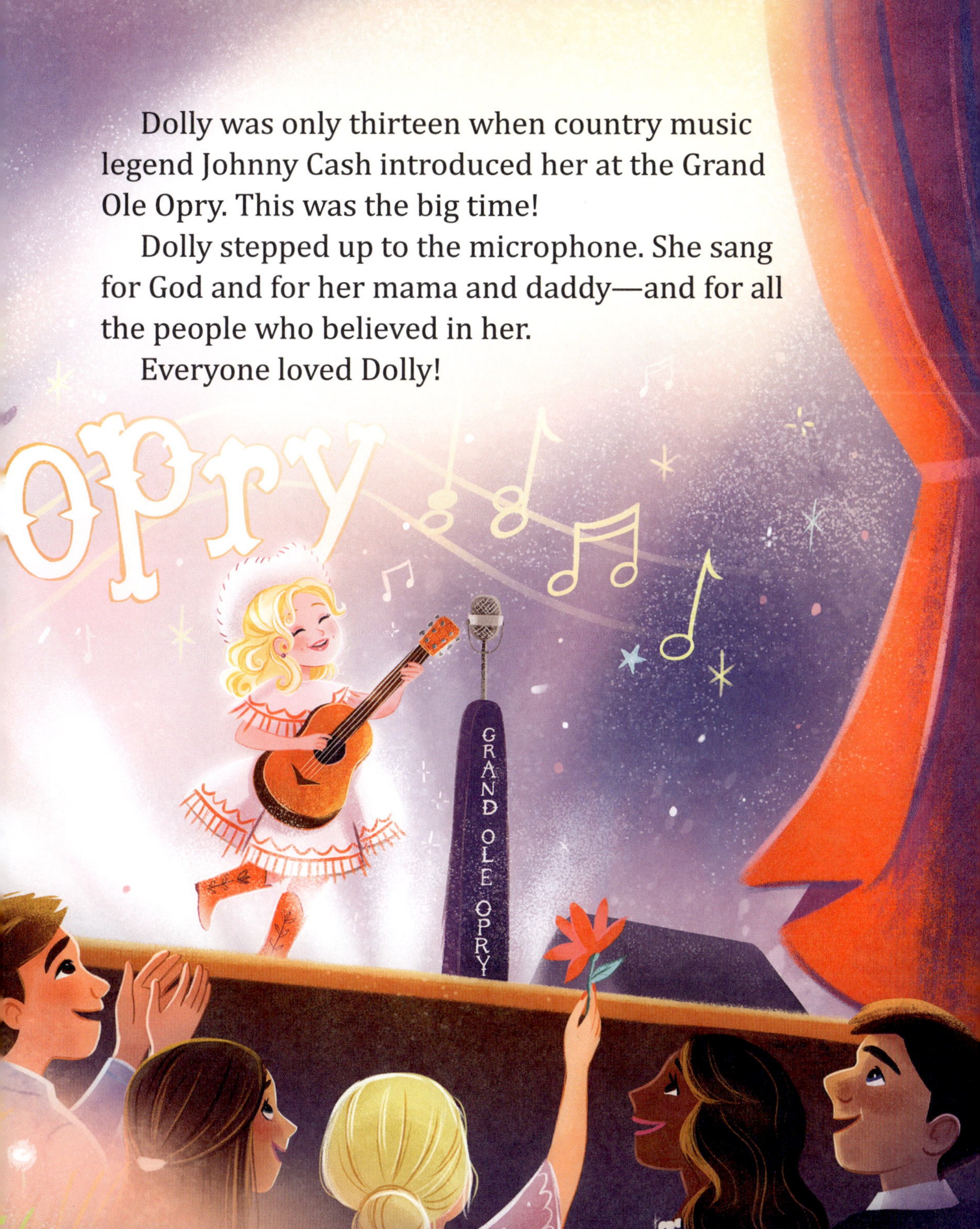

Dolly was only thirteen when country music legend Johnny Cash introduced her at the Grand Ole Opry. This was the big time!

Dolly stepped up to the microphone. She sang for God and for her mama and daddy—and for all the people who believed in her.

Everyone loved Dolly!

At her high school graduation, Dolly declared that she was going to Nashville to become a star. People laughed. But that only made her more determined to succeed.

The very next day, she hopped on a bus to Nashville with just her guitar, her songs, and a few belongings packed into three paper bags.

On her first day in town, outside the Wishy Washy Laundromat, Dolly met a handsome young man named Carl Dean. It was love at first sight.

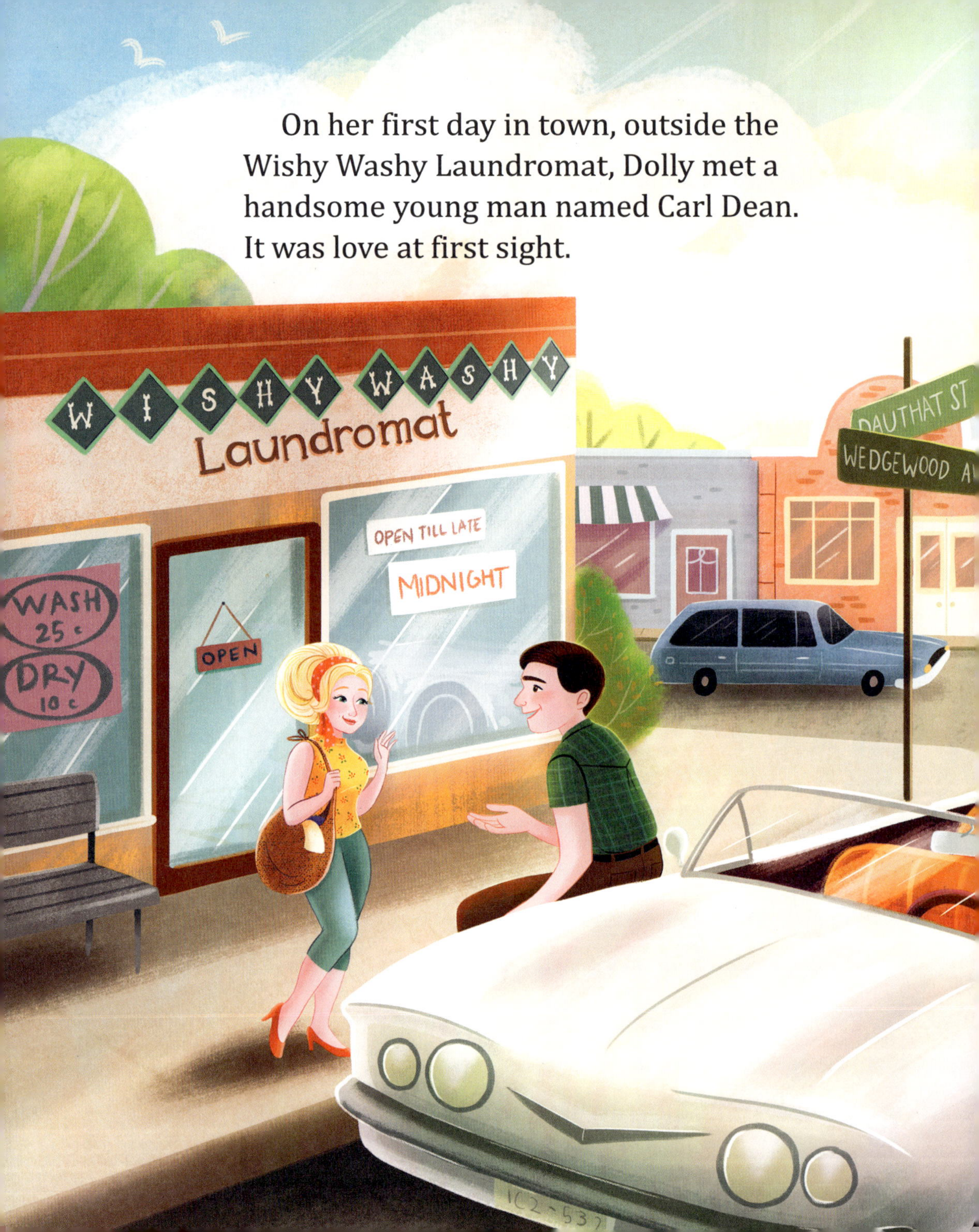

Two years later, Dolly and Carl decided to marry. They had a small, simple wedding and have been together ever since.

Although they never had children of their own, Dolly and Carl opened their hearts and home to help raise some of Dolly's younger brothers and sisters.

Years later, for their fiftieth wedding anniversary, Dolly and Carl decided to make up for their simple wedding. They married again, and this time, Dolly wore a shimmering gown. Then they got into their RV and went on a camping trip.

After Dolly and Carl first got married, Dolly kept working hard. Before long, some of her songs became number-one hits. She started to win big awards, including top female country singer of the year! But Dolly didn't limit herself to one kind of music. She made a big splash in pop music, too.

Since Dolly loved performing, one day she decided to try acting. Her first film, called *9 to 5,* is about women like her, who work hard for success. Dolly wrote the movie's title song, which became a huge hit.

Dolly never seems to run out of ideas—she has written more than five thousand songs!

It's no wonder Dolly's list of awards for songwriting, music, and acting fills many pages. She has changed country music. She has made television shows and written books, too. Dolly is one of the most honored American performers of all time.

Along with being a creative person, Dolly is a successful businesswoman. Each year, people flock to Dollywood, her theme park in the Smoky Mountains. Dollywood has brought jobs to the area, and it honors the music and traditions of the people who live there.

Dolly also helps in other ways. Out of love for her father, who never got the chance to learn to read, she began Dolly Parton's Imagination Library. Each month, Imagination Library sends free books to more than a million preschool children in America and in other countries around the world.

BEST STORIES

Like the butterfly she once followed as a child, Dolly has traveled far in her life. She began by singing on a woodpile. Now the whole world is her stage. She has never been afraid to be herself, or to raise her voice to help others.

Dolly Parton is like no one else. And one thing is certain:

Everyone loves Dolly!

DOLLY PARTON: One of a Kind!

Dolly is so much more than just a talented performer. She inspires people through her heartfelt songs, love of family and community, and dedication to helping others.

Turn the page to find out even more things to love about Dolly. . . .

The Dolly Quiz

How well do you know Dolly?

1. Which of these foods would Dolly happily eat every day?

    A. meatloaf

    B. potatoes

    C. spinach

    D. chicken pot pie

2. Which of these instruments does Dolly *not* play?

A. tuba
B. electric guitar
C. piano
D. saxophone

3. What is Dolly's favorite holiday?

A. Halloween
B. Thanksgiving
C. Christmas
D. New Year's Day

4. When Dolly isn't performing, which activity does she enjoy doing most?

A. swimming
B. golfing
C. bowling
D. reading

5. What did Dolly use as perfume when she was young?

A. vanilla extract
B. apple cider
C. honeysuckle flowers
D. rose oil

6. What did Dolly pack her clothes in when she moved to Nashville at age eighteen?

- A. a bright-red suitcase
- B. paper bags from the supermarket
- C. her father's duffel bag
- D. a yellow backpack with painted butterflies

7. Where does Dolly write a lot of her songs?

- A. on airplanes
- B. at her kitchen table
- C. in the bathtub
- D. all of the above

8. When traveling to shows early in her career, Dolly used the time on the tour bus to:

- A. Replace rhinestones on her costumes.
- B. Knit socks.
- C. Do crossword puzzles.
- D. Catch up on sleep.

9. What time does Dolly usually wake up?

- A. 3:00 a.m.
- B. 5:00 a.m.
- C. 7:00 a.m.
- D. 9:00 a.m.

10. What is Dolly's favorite thing to snack on at Dollywood?

A. cinnamon bread
B. pork rinds
C. funnel cake
D. cotton candy

No peeking!

The answers are on the next page. If you haven't finished the quiz yet, close your eyes, skip ahead *two* pages, then open your eyes so you can read more about Dolly.

Quiz Answers

1. B—Baked, mashed, or fried, Dolly loves potatoes!

2. A—Dolly can play at least eight different instruments, but the tuba is not one of them.

3. C—Dolly LOVES Christmas! She puts up her Christmas lights the day after Thanksgiving and doesn't take them down until her birthday on January 19!

4. D—Dolly is a big fan of reading. She has said, "When I'm all curled up and wrapped in my favorite blankets to read a book, it's as if the world does not exist to me."

5. C—Dolly would squash honeysuckle blossoms to make perfume.

6. B—In May 1964, Dolly boarded a Greyhound bus for Nashville with her clothes in paper bags from the Piggly Wiggly supermarket.

7. D—Dolly says she can write anywhere, anytime, and any place!

8. A—Putting rhinestones on things kept Dolly busy on the tour bus. She traveled with her own rhinestone repair kit.

9. A—Dolly is a very early riser! She likes to start her day at 3:00 a.m. with prayers, followed by writing, answering emails, and taking care of business.

10. C—Dolly enjoys eating a funnel cake when she visits her theme park.

Dolly was eighteen years old when she met Carl Dean outside the Wishy Washy Laundromat in Nashville. They ended up spending the next sixty years together!

Carl remembered thinking two things that day:

Lord, she's good-looking!

I'm gonna marry that girl.

“I wouldn’t be here if you hadn’t been there.”

After Carl passed away in 2025, Dolly wrote a song about their love story called “If You Hadn’t Been There.”

Song Starters

Dolly has written more than three thousand songs! Sometimes she writes about people and things from her imagination. Dolly once said, "In a song, I can go anywhere and do anything."

Write a song about going to a party on the moon.

Some of Dolly's songs, like "Coat of Many Colors," are about memories and events from her life.

Write a song about something you've experienced that made you happy.

Coats of Many Colors and Patterns

Dolly loved the coat her mama made her from different colorful scraps of fabric. Use crayons or colored pencils to design three special coats.

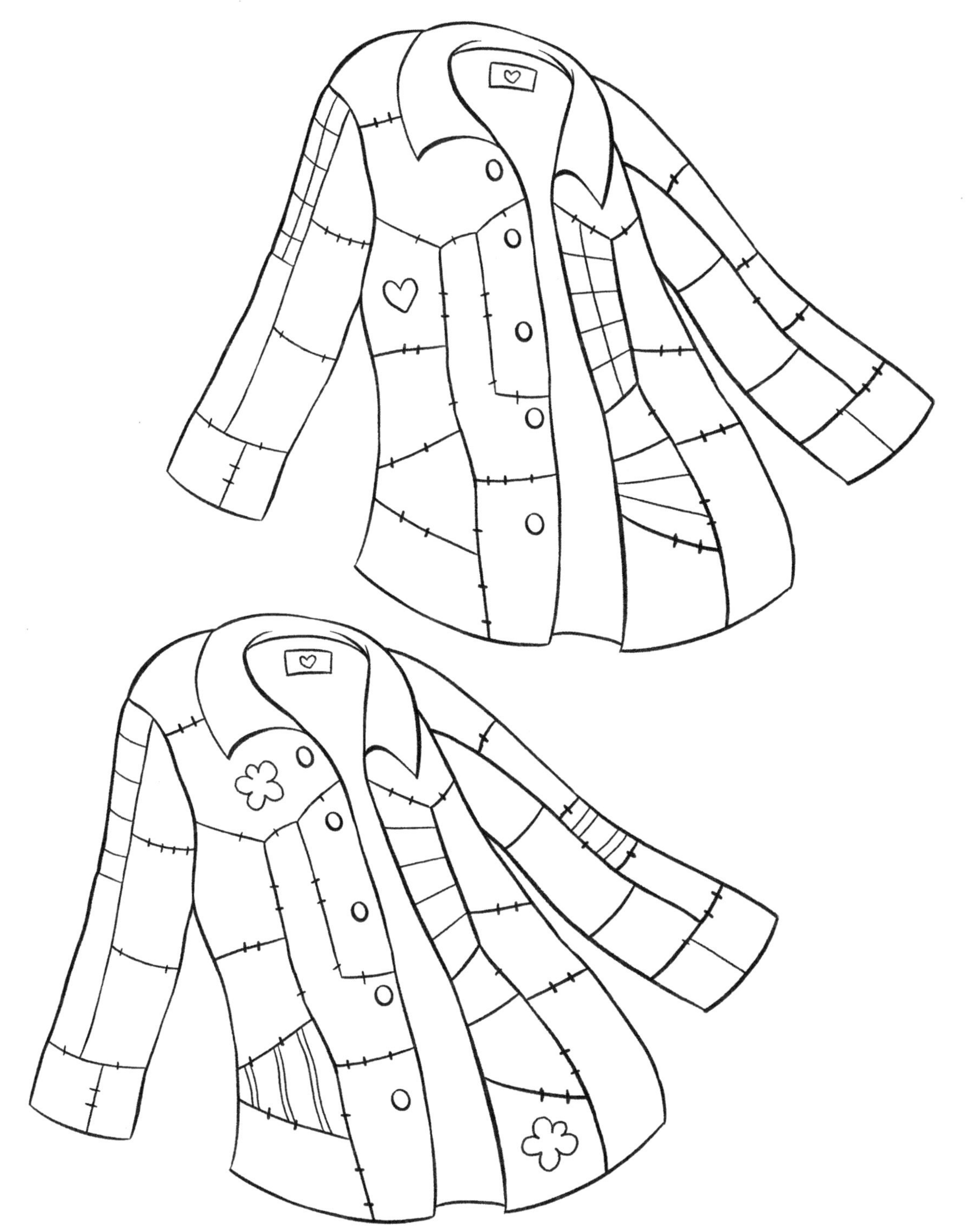

Making Music

Dolly is a country music star, but she doesn't just sing country music. From gospel and pop to Christmas tunes and rock, Dolly does it all!

Some of her songs, like "Here You Come Again" and "9 to 5," were on the country music chart and the pop music chart at the same time—these are called crossover hits. Dolly had a whole crossover album, too. *Rockstar* was the top album on the country music chart and the rock music chart.

Of all the songs she has recorded, Dolly has said "Down from Dover," "Coat of Many Colors," and "I Will Always Love You" are three of her favorites.

What are some of your favorite Dolly Parton songs?

1. ______________________________

2. ______________________________

3. ______________________________

4. ______________________________

5. ______________________________

Dolly enjoys singing with other talented musicians. Over the years, she has worked with country stars, rappers, rockers, and pop stars.

Some of her collaborations are "Islands in the Stream" with Kenny Rogers, "He's Everything" with Queen Latifah, "Everything's Beautiful (In Its Own Way)" with Willie Nelson, and "Please Please Please" with Sabrina Carpenter.

Who would you like Dolly to sing with?

____________________ ____________________

____________________ ____________________

Use crayons or colored pencils to
add your favorite colors to the pictures.

Dolly Gives Back

Dolly loves to encourage other people to dream more, learn more, care more, and *be more*. For Dolly, being more means being fair, generous, and compassionate to everybody.

Dollywood

Dolly founded Dollywood in Pigeon Forge, Tennessee in 1986 to provide much-needed jobs in the low-income area where she was raised. This super popular 165-acre theme park offers more than fifty rides and attractions. There's lots of great food and, of course, live music!

Dolly Parton's Imagination Library

In 1995, Dolly Parton's Imagination Library began sending free books every month to young children in Tennessee. Now the organization serves children across the United States and in several other countries, too, including Canada and Australia. By 2024, more than 255 million books had been given out to children under the age of five.

The first book Imagination Library sends to each child who registers is *The Little Engine That Could*. It's a book close to Dolly's heart. Just like the train in that story, Dolly has a can-do attitude—and she never, ever gives up!

Dolly Said It!

"If I'm remembered one hundred years from now, I hope it will not be for looks, but for **BOOKS**."

"I've never tried quitting, and **I never quit trying**."

"If you see **someone** without a **smile** today, give 'em **yours**."

"I'm a softie in my emotions, but I'm **strong** in my will."

"**Learning more** is all about taking chances."

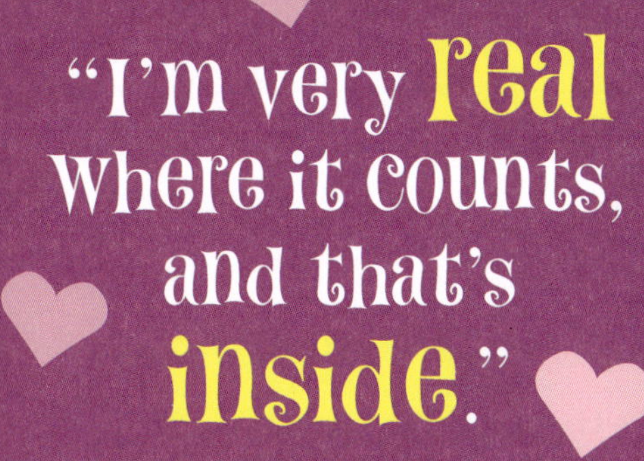

"They say
the early bird
gets the worm.
Well, they also
get a lot of
good ideas, too."

"You never
do a whole lot
unless you're
brave enough
to try."

"People always ask me
how long it takes
to do my hair.
**I don't know,
I'm never there**."

"I think everybody
should be allowed to
be who they are,
and to **love**
who they
love."

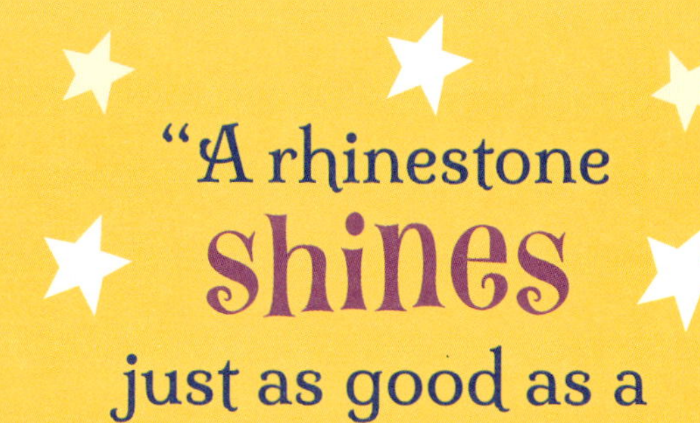

More to Come!

Dolly has a surprise for her fans to enjoy in the future!

She recorded a song and then locked it away in a time capsule. Dolly's Dream Box holds a piece of wood from the porch of the house she grew up in, a copy of her book *Dream More: Celebrate the Dreamer in You,* a CD with the secret song, and a CD player.

The box is set to be opened in 2045. No one will hear the song until then.

In 2045, Dolly will be ninety-nine years old. How old will you be?

DOLLY